"THE WORLD'S EASIEST POCKET GUIDE"

— TO —

Money
and
Marriage

"THE WORLD'S EASIEST POCKET GUIDE"

— TO —

Money
and
Marriage

LARRY BURKETT

WITH JEFF AND TEENA STEWART
ILLUSTRATED BY KEN SAVE

NORTHFIELD PUBLISHING

CHICAGO

Text & Illustrations © 2002 BURKETT & KIDS, LLC

Larry Burkett's Money Matters for Kids
Producer: *Allen Burkett*

For Lightwave Publishing
Managing Editor: *Rick Osborne*
Text Director: *Ed Strauss*
Desktop Publisher: *Andrew Jaster*

ISBN: 1-881273-53-9

1 3 5 7 9 10 8 6 4 2

Printed in the United States of America

Table of Contents

How to Use This Book

Shortly after leaving home, many young adults embark on a learning curve so drastic that it resembles a roller-coaster ride. Things they never did before—such as holding down a full-time job, paying bills, saving money, renting an apartment, using a credit card—suddenly become sink-or-swim survival skills. Most people fail to learn these basics while still at home and are woefully unprepared for life in the real world when they move out on their own.

The first four books in this series—*Getting Your First Credit Card, Buying Your First Car, Renting Your First Apartment,* and *Making Your First College Decision*—were written to teach you the basic life skills you need to survive in today's jungle. In the next four books, *Your First Full-Time Job, Your First Savings Plan, Planning Your First Investment,* and *Creating Your First Financial Plan,* we walked you step-by-step through getting and keeping a job, saving money, investing money, and getting and keeping control of your money.

In these four new books, *Personal Budgeting, Buying Your First House, Money and Marriage,* and *Buying Insurance,* we teach you how to pay your bills and have money left over, walk through the maze of house buying, get married without going in debt, and buy the insurance you need.

These books contain a wealth of commonsense tips. They also give sound advice from a godly, biblical perspective. It is our prayer that the books in this series will save you from having to learn these things in the "school of hard knocks."

To get the most out of these books, you should photocopy and complete the checklists and forms we've included. We provided them to help you take on these new tasks step-by-step and to make these books as practical as possible.

Each book contains a glossary to explain commonly used terms. If at any point while reading you need a clear definition of a certain word or term, you can look it up. Each book also contains a helpful index that allows you to find pages where a key word or subject is mentioned in the book.

CHAPTER 1

A Lifelong Commitment

"I remember when I first began to realize that there was something different about this guy . . ."

"I really am beginning to think he may be the one . . ."

A Lifelong Commitment

Jenny and Kenny

Jenny was trembling as Karen, her maid of honor, helped place the wedding veil on top of Jenny's meticulously styled chestnut tresses. Jenny's strange reflection stared back from the mirror on the church's nursery wall. *Is this really me?* She hardly recognized herself under all the makeup and hair spray. She mentally calculated the money she'd spent during the last twenty-four hours—fake nails and complete manicure at the nail salon, new hairstyle and highlights at the beauty parlor, gifts for the bridesmaids, a check for the wedding planner, a check to the pastor and to the musicians . . . She pushed the thoughts of these and many other recent expenses to the back of her mind. It was *worth* it.

Jenny wanted this day to be absolutely perfect. Not a hair of her carefully coiffured head was out of place. She'd spent an hour at the hairdresser's that morning and made sure that before she stepped out of the salon her hair was protected with a heavy coat of hair spray. Karen reached up and adjusted Jenny's veil and laughed. "Even if a hurricane blew through the sanctuary, your hair won't budge." The roomful of primping bridesmaids laughed.

"Just think Jenny," she added, "in just a few more minutes you'll be Mrs. Kenny Parker!" The knot that had been in Jenny's stomach all morning tightened, and a cold feeling rushed over her. The room was starting to tilt. She sat down hard in a nearby chair and put her head between her knees.

Karen chatted away, oblivious to her about to be sister-in-law's condition. "Whew! You'll never know how close this wedding came to *not happening!*"

Jenny lifted her head slowly as Kenny's sister rambled on. "At the last minute Kenny's new credit card arrived in the mail."

"Whaaat?" said Jenny, her eyes widening.

"Didn't Kenny tell you? He'd already maxed out all five of his credit cards. He owes about one hundred thousand. So if the new card hadn't arrived . . . *Well!* We won't even think about *that.*

And the honeymoon, I think he borrowed the money from a loan shark, but don't worry. After you get married, you can both get second jobs delivering pizza at night to pay it back before the penalty period hits with 40 percent interest!"

There was a knock on the door. One of the bridesmaids opened it a crack, enough for the pastor to poke his head into the nursery. He smiled and looked at Jenny. "Are you ready?"

Jenny's pale face washed out completely as she slowly slid onto the floor.

While this story may not be the state of *your* upcoming marriage, it's unfortunately not far off the mark for many young people.

"A" Wedding Versus "the" Marriage

Many young men and women set out to duplicate the dream-like fairy tales they've seen in movies and read about in books, spending unimaginable amounts of money in the process. But marriage is more than passionate physical attraction and the picture-perfect ceremony. What the movies and books never reveal is what happens the morning after when Cinderella and Prince Charming wake up with buffalo breath and bed hair. Marriage is not a fairy tale. It is real and it is work.

A wedding serves as a symbol, a starting point for your entire marriage, whereas marriage gets below the surface. A wedding is a short-term—and often very extravagant—expense, whereas marriage is a long-term, major investment. To have a successful marriage requires discipline and the highest degree of commitment. We're living in an age when 43 percent of new marriages are expected to end in divorce (Divorce and Marriage Statistics—http://www.aamft.org/Press_Room/Press_releases/stats.htm). Since 80 percent of these divorces are caused by financial problems, having a clear understanding of fundamental financial principles is key to building a strong marriage.

Homes *and* Marriages Are Investments

What you do today to prepare for both your wedding and your marriage will stay with you for a very long time. That's why it's so important to make careful choices now. The thought of writing a 30-year mortgage on a three-bedroom house every month for three full decades is more than a little intimidating. Well! A life-long marriage exceeds three decades and costs even *more*.

Wise people who are looking to purchase a house don't let a salesman's charm sucker them into making a poor choice. Houses aren't cheap and after you're in a home you spend most of the rest of your life paying for it and improving on it. If you do your homework carefully, you choose a home that will serve as a safe abode and will appreciate in value—something you'll cherish for years to come. You save for a down payment, take out loans, and have the property inspected to make sure it's sound. Once you consider all of the responsibility and are sure you have the resources in place, you make the commitment. You do so with the knowledge that in order to keep something this valuable and help it appreciate, you must continually work to *maintain* and *improve* the investment.

If couples put in as much time and preparation into their marriage commitment as they do into home ownership, imagine the difference it would make in the marriage failure rate. How well do you know your partner and his or her values? Do you trust your partner completely? Is your future mate capable of wise and reliable financial decisions?

In essence, you're an investor and wise investors do their homework before taking the plunge. Wise investors also know that following their commitment they must continually *work* on improving their investment—in this case, your marital relationship and finances.

Commitment and Investment

These days, a marriage that lasts twenty-five years or more is a novelty. Recently, a single young man learned of Jeff and Teena's approaching 25th wedding anniversary. Curious, he asked them to share their secret for marital success. They explained there had been both smooth and rocky times in their marriage, but their commitment and willingness to invest the time and effort to make it work helped establish a solid, healthy relationship. After twenty-five years, they remain best friends because of their willingness to work on their relationship. Their response centered around two key words: *commitment* and *investment.*

When we are committed it means we have every intention of seeing something through, even when the going gets rough. When we invest in something, it means we will make the added effort to study and learn how to make it work.

The Beginning of the Investment

Weddings are surface symbols of the deep unity that comes through marriage. Marriage reveals our true selves. It's where the real work begins. This book will give you sound advice for avoiding many of the financial pitfalls many young couples encounter and will challenge you to begin financial disciplines, enabling you to have a festive wedding day and provide you with resources for carrying these principles over into marriage.

Books, magazines, and other resources list the many wedding details you'll want to attend to as you plan your wedding. But just remember, a builder never begins work on a structure without doing preliminary work—hiring an architect, surveying the land, or figuring out expenses. Many couples are so focused on outer details they fail to attend to the *deeper* issues such as getting premarital counseling or doing the basic math on how much their wedding and marriage will cost.

It's hard to believe but the average cost of a wedding today is $20,000. If you don't pay for it *before* you wed, you'll pay for it after, along with other financial responsibilities you and your partner will share like school loans, car loans, etc. So let's put money before marriage.

Counting the Cost

Marriage is a major paradigm shift. There is a lifelong learning curve involved. That's why both partners need to be not only committed but have their eyes open as they go into *a* ceremony that commences *the* lifelong relationship. Jesus spoke about estimating the cost before becoming His disciple: "Suppose one of you wants to build a tower. Will he not first sit down and estimate the cost to see if he has enough money to complete it? In the same way, any of you who does not give up everything he has cannot be my disciple" (Luke 14:28, 33). Giving up everything you have means *total* commitment.

In Ephesians 5:21–33, Paul compares marriage to the same type of self-denying commitment required of discipleship. The whole passage is kicked off with, "Submit to one another out of reverence for Christ" (verse 21). Both the husband and wife are directed to serve their spouse with humility. It's interesting to note that the man has two times as many verses addressed to him as the woman does—six compared to three. Paul must have realized that guys don't *get* it until they've been told more than once. (OK, OK, just kidding, but the point is: a successful marriage takes both commitment and humility.)

Start "Stashing the Cash"

Now that we've looked at some of the deeper, underlying issues, let's look at actual wedding costs, shall we? Maybe all this talk about cost has rattled you. The fact is, though, most weddings *are* too extravagant. People saddle themselves with debt by throwing a megabash that they're still paying for years later. As stated before, the average cost for a wedding is a whopping $20,000. That includes not only the invitation cards but the wedding dress, bridesmaids' dresses, tuxedos, flowers, photographers, wedding cake, and on and on.

The *most* expensive part of the wedding is the reception that follows the ceremony. For two hundred guests, for hall rental, food, and catering, you may pay over $8,000! The *second* biggest expense is the engagement ring, which can cost up to $3,000. And guess what? That $20,000 total doesn't even include the honeymoon! That adds thousands more dollars to the price tag!

A lot of young couples start down the road of debt together before they even say, "I do." Fully 80 percent of all divorces today are caused by financial problems and far too many marriage breakups begin with the wedding itself. You can cut costs from your wedding by trimming your guest list and other expenses. This will be covered in chapter 5. But just the same, your wedding—and getting set up as newlyweds—is *still* going to be expensive, and you need to start saving for these expenses today.

CHAPTER 2

Priorities and Commitments

"I'm just crazy about her and I don't think I can wait! I wanna get married now!"

"Look, you've got one year of college left. Put that first, then get married. marriage and everything else that goes with it, you might not be able to get the kind of job you'll need to support your family in the future."

Priorities and Commitments

No Mon, No Fun, Hon

For the fourth night in a row, Jan and Tom sat down to a scrumptious meal of hot dogs. Monday it was hot dogs on buns. Tuesday it was hot dogs and canned chili. Wednesday night it was Beanie Weenies, a delectable delicacy of chopped hot dogs and pork and beans; tonight it was tube steaks without buns. They didn't even have enough dough to buy bread. They pulled up their mismatched chairs to the battered dinette and began to eat in silence.

Another Friday night and they were stuck at home again, too broke to even rent a video. Besides, the last video they'd rented was still caught in the machine, which displayed an appetite lately for gobbling up whatever they tried to watch. They didn't have the money to get it fixed. How would they pay for the late fee on the video? Six months of marriage . . . both working two jobs to pay off all those bills they'd run up over the wedding. *If I'd only known what we were getting into,* thought Tom, as he pushed a ketchup-smothered hot dog around on his plate.

Across the table Jan saw her own weary feelings mirrored in her husband's face. She wanted to tell him what she'd found out at the doctor's today but she couldn't work up the nerve. *How would they ever pay for another mouth to feed?*

You may not be in Jan's and Tom's shoes, but scenarios like this do happen to young couples across America. Before marriage all they can think about is how much they're in love, and all the way to the altar they're humming lines from old Beatles' songs, like, "love is *all* you need" and "money can't buy you love." Well, the Beatles were *millionaires* when they wrote, "love is all you need," and while money can't buy you love, it *does* keep men and women alive so they can keep on loving. So let's look at getting your finances in shape *before* you get married.

Reality Check

As you consider your marriage, put the proverbial horse in front of the cart where it belongs: put your finances and your educational/career-oriented goals first! We're not talking about being materialistic. We're talking about responsibility and common sense. Of course your relationship, more than anything, must be founded upon the solid rock of loving God and trusting Him. If you depend on money for your happiness, your focus and heart are in the wrong place and your marriage will suffer. On the other hand, entering marriage with little or no financial preparation will create a lot of strain on the relationship too.

After you marry, your first challenge will be switching from the "me" to "us" mentality since you'll be responsible for meeting your own needs plus those of your partner. You (plural) will decide where to live, how to budget your money, even what kind of tissues to buy. Your (plural) total income will determine how well you'll be able meet daily expenses. Keep in mind that your income will also need to cover life insurance, health benefits, and allow plans for the cost of expanding your family. Ideally, you should be able to pay bills, invest for the future, and have money left over for fun. How do you do all that? Read on!

Make Your Preparations First

Proverbs 24:27 advises us, "Finish your outdoor work and get your fields ready; *after that,* build your house." Before you establish a household with your marriage partner, you need to first work in the "fields" making preparations for your future. This is a clear reference to getting a job, working hard, and getting your finances in place first.

This type of discipline doesn't come naturally for many couples. Don't let the temptation to bring on the "big day" in a hurry keep you from making wise decisions regarding finances now. When you're seriously contemplating marriage, *prepare*. It takes patience to wait for certain privileges, and it takes persistence—lifelong habits of self-discipline—to provide for your family and pay all the bills after marriage.

Discipline is not a common virtue today. With the radio waves filling their heads with one-sided ideas of love, people put off preparedness and rush in on pleasure. *Think* about it: When was the last time you heard a love song that said, "I'm saving up my money, honey; I'm holding my love in check. I'm waiting for that day while I save away, 'cause I don't want to live in debt." Contrary to the Top Ten, feelings and romance are not the only factors, nor is your need for physical love. Before you rush to bring on the big day, there are several practical considerations to take care of.

Start by Getting a Good Job

Before starting life together, one of the wisest steps you can make is to "get your fields ready." That means establishing a firm financial base for you and your spouse, and that means securing a good job. But before you can enter the career of your choice, you'll need specific education and skills.

Maybe you already have a clear-cut idea of what you want to do for a living. You may even have a job. Did you realize there is a difference between a job and a career? A job is what you do to earn income, often for minimum pay with little chance for advancement. A career allows you to not only use your gifts and skills but to also learn new skills—and has opportunity for advancement. So don't settle down for life in the first paying position you find. Look at the big picture. You need a good job with good benefits (medical, dental, etc.) to support a spouse and family.

Having career goals is very important. It shows that you're thinking ahead, but don't expect to reach great heights and wages when just starting out. Take it one step at a time, figuring out what you need to do to reach your goals.

Many companies offer free courses with on-the-job training that provide new skills and advancement opportunities. You may want to explore internships in your field of interest. Do you know someone with a skill you'd like to learn? Perhaps they would let you apprentice with them. Also, trade schools specialize in technical and mechanical know-how, require fewer years, and are usually less expensive than college, plus provide you with hands-on training.

When you're ready to take steps toward your career, keep factors and issues in mind such as rate of pay, benefits, salary reviews, commuting distance, and company/industry reputation. (For more information, read the book in this series, *Your First Full-Time Job.*)

Building upon Your Education

It's the norm to expect high school grads to go to college, but in many cases people aren't ready or even suited for college. That's why you often see college students either wasting their time on wild parties or graduates asking burger patrons: "Would you like to super-size that order?"

Give careful consideration to God's direction for your life. Sometimes it's wise to wait before continuing your education. What's the hurry? You might want to take a year off before going to college. Waiting can be a good thing because it allows new opportunities to open up. You might even consider setting a long-range marriage date so you can work and save for your future while you plan and investigate your life career.

There are many tools and strategies to explore as you progress through your educational and/or career goals. If college is still your top choice, look for as many ways as possible to save money to pay for it ahead of time. Check into scholarships and grants. And search locally. Consider a work-study program or work and pay as you go. If you apply for loans, make that a very last resort. If you can avoid any loans, your financial and emotional burdens after graduating will be *much* less.

Education and Career Inventory

Do get an education or some type of quality training if you genuinely need it to get into your life's career and a job that pays the bills. You may need more education to get to the career level you want but don't be locked into the idea of college. College is the most expensive route and can leave you with years of debt. More importantly, it's not for everybody.

Take the time to evaluate your current situation and critique your perspective. Perhaps you haven't expanded your focus beyond your present job. Do you really like what you're doing or is it a downer? Are you adequately compensated for what you put into your work? Are you using the natural gifts and abilities God has given you? Use this helpful survey below to determine where you are and where you want to be and could be, and then list the steps needed to get you there.

Present job_____

Satisfaction with Work
- Love it.
- It's not that great but pays the bills.
- I'd have more fun cleaning horse stalls.

How's the Pay?
- Great pay. I really can't complain.
- Pretty standard for the kind of work I do.
- My boss is Ebenezer Scrooge!

My strongest gifts/talents/skills _____
Duties and responsibilities of my ideal job _____
What kind of career I feel God calling me to _____

What steps (education/training) must I take to reach my final career goal? How long will each step take and how much will it cost me?

Steps	Time	Cost	
Education: _____			$ ____
Training: _____			$ ____
Starting position: __ _____			
Secondary position: _____			
Final position: _____			

CHAPTER 3

Attitudes Toward Stewardship

Attitudes Toward Stewardship

Do Your Life Goals Match?

Any couple going into marriage needs to sit down and have a heart-to-heart talk to make sure that their objectives and goals for their lives match. Does one of you want to be a missionary and the other one want to put down roots in Hometown, USA? Are your partner's *attitudes* on life and *approach* to life similar to yours? Does one want to enjoy the good life, while the other wants to give it all away? Is one thrifty while the other one lives from paycheck to paycheck, blowing money on outings and gifts? Do you have the same outlook toward earning money, spending it, saving it, and giving to God?

In Las Vegas it isn't unheard of for a couple to meet, drop in at a chapel, have Elvis escort them down the aisle, and tie the knot all in a very short time for a minimal price. You can bet that in less than a year's time, many of these marriages are in the doghouse with both partners singing, "You ain't nothin' but a houn' dog." Why? Because these couples didn't take time to really get to know each other.

Premartial counseling helps lay a good foundation. It can reveal compatibility, fundamental spiritual beliefs, conflict management styles—even totally different philosophies about handling money and finances. Finding out this kind of thing now will prevent heartaches later. Count yourself fortunate if you attend a church where the pastor insists that you both take premarital counseling before he consents to marry you.

Where Do You Stand?

Are you and your partner committed to following and living God's Word? Do you attend church on a regular basis? How about your partner? Be very careful not to brush aside spiritual differences. Don't think, "Ah . . . our love is so strong it will overcome all differences." The small cracks you notice now can become enormous chasms later. Don't sweep them under the carpet. Have a heart-to-heart talk about these issues. Now.

Remember the fairy tale where an evil enchantress turned a handsome prince into a frog? Along came a princess who had only to kiss the frog prince to break the spell and return him to his princely form. Couples often enter into marriage with fairy-tale expectations: they expect the frog they marry to be transformed after marriage and are surprised when, after repeated kisses, they find they have indeed married a frog . . . and nothing more.

If there are issues that concern you regarding your partner-to-be *before* marriage, don't expect these concerns to simply vanish *after* marriage. They are what they are, warts and all. What he or she believes *now* will carry over after you exchange wedding vows, so you'd better be ready to deal with those issues on a daily basis. This is why God's Word warns: "Do not be yoked together with unbelievers" (2 Corinthians 6:14). And being married is about as *yoked* as you can get.

If you're basing your decisions on Christ's teachings and your partner has a different perspective, you'll be pulled in two different directions. Marriage to an unbeliever can also drag the believer away from Christian fellowship. Think of the case (and there are plenty of them) where one partner gets up every Sunday morning to go to church and the other partner sleeps in. That's a mild example. Sometimes unbelieving spouses are hostile and antagonistic to their Christian spouses. When this happens, many people throw up their hands and give up their convictions in order to keep peace in the marriage.

Merging Two into One

God often puts opposite personality types together in a marriage, not to frustrate them but to allow the strengths of one spouse to balance the weaknesses of the other. Marrying an opposite has its benefits. It *also* creates more work, since personality differences you notice before marriage are often magnified *after* marriage.

Your personality dictates how you respond to people and circumstances. This, coupled with family upbringing, plays into your attitude toward money management. You may find that you and your partner handle money quite differently. You may discover that your partner has never saved a penny in his or her life. In fact, he or she may have thousands of dollars in debts—debts that you will also become liable for if you marry him or her. These are things you would want to *know* about before saying, "I do."

To avoid financial and marital problems later on, here are some scriptural principles you both should agree on.

We Are Called to Stewardship

A steward is someone who is in charge of managing someone else's resources. Since God owns the world and everything in it—including *us*—then whatever things we "own" really belong to God. Thus, we are obligated to manage God's belongings in the ways God has set out in His Word. You may argue, "It's my money. I was the one who worked hard and earned it." Deuteronomy 8:17–18 cautions, "You may say to yourself, '*My* power and the strength of *my* hands have produced this wealth for me.' But remember the Lord your God, for it is *he* who gives you the ability to produce wealth."

Why is it important to have a proper attitude of stewardship? For one, it causes you to be dependent on God and therefore opens your life up to His guidance and His blessing. For another, it makes it easier for you to obey the financial principles in His Word. The way people handle money usually is a good thermometer reading of their inner values. "For where your treasure is, there your heart will be also" (Matthew 6:21).

And finally, having a stewardship mind-set creates a thankful attitude, which is crucial if you are to faithfully give to God in appreciation for all that He has given you. As King David acknowledged, "Everything comes from you, and we have given you only what comes from your hand" (1 Chronicles 29:14). Do you and your partner embrace this important principle?

We Should Give to God

In the Bible, the first tenth was given to God in acknowledgment that He was the true owner of their property and resources. When we give first of all to God, before paying any of our other bills, we show that we acknowledge God's ownership over every-thing. Because giving involves money, however, it can cause friction between a husband and wife. That's why it's best to hammer out this detail before you *become* husband and wife. Whether you give 5 percent, 10 percent, or 15 percent, as a Christian you are obligated to *give*. God asks His people to give generously and cheerfully from the heart (2 Corinthians 9:6–7).

Committed giving is important, but you should be in agreement. Have you discussed the amount you will give to church, charity, and missions after you're married? Do you want to give 10 percent while your mate would rather give 5 percent? Talk it over. Pray over it as well. Ask God for His wisdom in setting the amount. If afterwards your mate is still reluctant to give the amount you desire, agree with the lower amount for now. God honors the intent of your heart (2 Corinthians 8:12).

Say No to Secret Spending

It's a temptation for couples to secretly spend money on things if they want those things bad enough and know their spouse would disagree with the expenditure. Some husbands like to go golfing when their budget can't afford it. A wife might habitually buy new clothes and, if she's the one handling the finances, make sure that her husband doesn't find out how much she spent.

When you're married, one thing you simply *must* be is completely open and honest with finances. Say no to secret spending! It is divisive and dishonest and leads to cover-ups and outright lies. Now, if the man *really* likes an occasional game of golf and the woman really *needs* new clothes from time to time, they should discuss these . . . er . . . "needs," agree on them, and write them into their budget. Couples should give each other an allowance if they must, but whatever they do, do it openly and honestly.

Ours, Not Mine

After you marry you'll be working as a team. It makes sense for the person who is more capable with managing money to handle the finances. This includes paying bills and balancing the checkbook. If you can possibly decide on this *before* marriage, it will make things run much more smoothly later. If not, it'll soon become clear who is best suited to manage the money. If your spouse says, "Hey, we can afford that! I have $1,000 of wiggle room left on my credit card," it's an indicator that you need to step in.

Don't forget to discuss where you will hold your bank accounts and the types of accounts you will have. There is a tendency to want to maintain your own checking/savings accounts after marriage, but God's perfect plan is for you to combine your resources. Separate accounts promote selfishness and hoarding. Merging your accounts reveals your faith in the Lord and—very importantly—in your spouse. If you truly don't trust that person with your money, chances are you shouldn't marry him or her.

Start Planning and Set Goals

"I'll think about it tomorrow," said Scarlett O'Hara *(Gone with the Wind)* when faced with a tough decision. You're young and in love and the last thing on your mind might be financial planning. But this is a *must-do*. It's not too early (before marriage) to begin setting both short-range and long-range goals. Start by sharing your dreams with each other. It doesn't cost anything to dream.

If you wish to buy a home or go overseas as short-term missionaries, discuss those dreams together and write them down on a sheet of paper. Then beside each goal, write how much it will cost in dollars and cents to make each one happen and how long it will take to save that money. Keep this on hand as a checklist, which you can check off as you accomplish each goal—or a tally sheet, to let you know how much you've saved to date. (For the full scoop on doing this, see *Creating Your First Financial Plan,* another book in this series.)

Setting goals will help you and your partner work together for a common purpose. It will also help you work past differences and draw you closer together. When you're forced to tighten the belt or curtail an evening out, remind each other, "We're making this sacrifice in order to reach that big goal we both want so badly."

Prenuptial Agreements

With all this talk about coming to important agreements before marriage, let's make one thing clear: we are *not* talking about prenuptial agreements. More and more couples are opting for legal contracts specifying the conditions of their marriage and how property will be divided should it fail. But successful marriages need both *trust* and *commitment*. Though prenuptial agreements are intended to protect couples and ensure their welfare, they can turn on the tap to dissension and distrust. They leave little room for forgiveness and can be an "easy out" for couples who'd rather call it quits than try to put in the effort to work things out.

Those who agree to "prenups" are more likely to treat marriage as a surface commitment (a form of bondage) than a serious covenant (to do what it takes to make it work). If people enter marriage with the mind-set that marriage is not a revolving door but a lifetime commitment, they increase their chances of success. (Remember the old Huey Lewis and the News song, "Happy to Be Stuck with You"?)

How Well Do You Know Your Future Mate?

Schedule time to sit down with your fiancé to discuss your convictions on financial matters. Read each point together, then pause to discuss your reactions to it before reading the next one.

1. I carefully plan my purchases and rarely buy on impulse.
2. I put money aside in savings from each paycheck.
3. Money talks but all mine usually says is "good-bye."
4. I am good with math and have no trouble balancing my checkbook.
5. I don't have the slightest clue how to balance a checkbook.
6. I have debts that I'm responsible to pay.
7. I always pay off any credit cards at the end of each month.
8. I owe $___ in credit card debts and pay __% interest on those debts. I've had these debts for __months/__years.
9. Sometimes I am late paying my bills, or forget to pay them.
10. I frequently buy new clothes/eat out because it makes me feel good.

11. I have saved $___ for our wedding and married life together.
12. I value quality over bargains and don't mind spending a little more.
13. I could probably wring a dollar out of a nickel because I'm superthrifty.
14. I have a place for everything and always put things where they belong.
15. I'm . . . well, a little messy and sometimes misplace bills, warranties, etc.
16. I don't think overspending and being in debt is any big deal.
17. I play the lotto. I believe I'll win big some day.
18. I am goal oriented and like to plan what happens next.
19. I frequently use lists to remind me of activities and chores.
20. I believe Jesus is God's Son and He died for me.
21. I base my decisions on Jesus' teachings and try to model my life after Him.
22. I attend church often/occasionally/almost never.
23. I read my Bible and have personal devotions on my own.
24. I am a different denomination from my fiancé but am open to changing.
25. I haven't given much thought to having children.
26. Have children? Whatever—I guess one or two might be all right.
27. I would like to put career first for a few years before raising a family.

Be Sure You Agree on the Following Points

- Whether all money will be shared and all accounts combined
- Who is best suited to handling finances
- That your money belongs to God and you are His money managers
- Your financial goals and dreams
- How much you give faithfully to your church
- That your main life goals are consistent (one doesn't want to be a missionary while the other wants to settle down in their hometown)
- There will be no secret spending, but all financial decisions will be discussed and agreed upon

CHAPTER 4

A Fresh Start

"Isn't he just so . . . wonderful . . . taking another job to make sure that his college loan is all paid off before we get married."

A Fresh Start

Marrying into Debt

A young woman wrote to a financial planner, concerned about her fiancé's poor credit. Her credit rating was excellent because she paid her debts faithfully, but her fiancé was another story. He never paid his bills on time, and she had to frequently remind him of what was due. She understood that marriage would change their financial management methods from "mine" to "ours" and was worried because she didn't want to be responsible for his debts. The financial planner pointed out that marriage *would* make her responsible for her fiancé's debt and spending habits, so unless she kept all of her assets (even their home) under her name only, she would share responsibility for his debts.

As a married couple you will share everything, including finances. If either of you has a sizable debt, it won't go away after marriage. It would be a wise move to enroll in a debt management class or see a financial counselor who can help you get a handle on your debts. (Talk with knowledgeable Christians or contact Crown Financial Ministries.) *Now* is the time to begin working on debt. If you feel your spouse has some maturing to do in this area, then why rush the wedding? Take some time to work things through.

The less baggage you bring with you, the less stress there will be and the stronger your marriage will be. What debts do you and your fiancé presently have? Are you paying off huge credit card debts? Are you paying off your college loan? Are your spending habits *still* completely out of control?

Should Debtors Marry?

When your brain is dumping gallons of "love hormones" into your bloodstream—dopamine, norepinephrine, and neuropeptide oxytocin—you may feel so "in love" that you of *course* should marry him or her no matter *how* high the debts are. But after you're married and your brain turns off the hormones, cold hard reality hits and you're left with years of stress and self-sacrifice as you pay bills together. This can put a *tremendous* strain on even the most loving relationships, and your brain will no longer be pumping out dopamine to sweeten the experience.

Making monthly payments on a car is no reason to postpone your wedding. However, if one or both of you have a huge college loan to pay and interest is building up as we speak—or if either of you has large credit card debts—you should seriously consider postponing the big day. And if one of you *still* has uncontrolled spending habits, you should seriously think of calling off the marriage entirely.

To strike a balance, telling people to put off marriage for ten years until they can pay off a college loan is a little unrealistic. To avoid sexual immorality, "each man should have his own wife, and each woman her own husband" (1 Corinthians 7:2). If you simply *must* get married, (1) get serious financial counseling beforehand, (2) rein in and change your spending habits, (3) commit to a realistic repayment plan, (4) go into such a marriage with your eyes open, knowing that finances will be tight and self-sacrifice will be required.

Common Pitfalls That Lead to Debt

Having a credit mentality gives couples the ability to borrow and allows them to buy things they can't afford. In their early years of marriage, couples are particularly at risk because buying on credit allows them to accumulate a lot of *things* that older married couples have. As a young married couple, Teena and Jeff were once so anxious to buy a new couch they purchased one on credit, planning to pay it off in a matter of months. But finances were tight and the months turned into years. It taught them a valuable lesson. By the time they'd finished paying for that couch, it was *well* past new. The finance charges alone could have purchased yet another couch. Impatience to "have it now" cost them hundreds more than the actual value of the couch.

Buying a Car

Many young couples already *have* cars before they marry. Automobiles are the second biggest purchases. Buying a new car can be a major trap for couples, especially those with a tendency to overspend—because they're generally not concerned with the overall price of the car, just the amount of the monthly payments.

Saving in order to purchase a good *used* car is wiser than financing or purchasing a new car. A new car costs more in taxes, insurance, and monthly payments than one that's even one year older. The minute you drive a new car off the lot, it loses value. If both you and your fiancé are paying car payments, you can save money by selling one of them and paying off your loan.

How to Avoid These Pitfalls

Use the form below to identify every single debt that each of you presently have. Later on this information will be used to help you create your first budget. It will also ensure there are no surprise confessions of debt after the honeymoon. List all debts and obligations, rounding them out to the nearest dollar amount. Also write out how much the monthly payment is on each one. If a payment is past due, make a note of that.

Debt Work Sheet

His			Hers	
Amount owed	Payment		Amount owed	Payment
_____	_____	Car	_____	_____
_____	_____	Car Insurance	_____	_____
_____	_____	Child Support	_____	_____
_____	_____	Clothes	_____	_____
_____	_____	Credit Card(s)	_____	_____
_____	_____		_____	_____
_____	_____	Loans	_____	_____
_____	_____		_____	_____
_____	_____	Medical	_____	_____
_____	_____	Taxes	_____	_____
_____	_____	Wedding	_____	_____
Total Debt	Total Monthly Debt		Total Debt	Total Monthly Debt
_____	_____		_____	_____

CHAPTER 5

Saving for Your Wedding

Saving for Your Wedding

Spending a Fortune on a Show

Two 1990s movies show how weddings have progressed from simple to complex, inexpensive to megabucks. In *Little Women,* Meg, the oldest of the four March girls, is married during the Civil War era in a simple ceremony under an arbor in the family's back yard. Following the ceremony the small group of friends and family members encircle the bride and groom, singing a hymn. The joy and laughter continues at the reception, a simple picnic of homemade cake and food served outdoors.

Compare this to the movie *Father of the Bride,* where the father, portrayed by Steve Martin, nearly has a breakdown because of the cost of his daughter's elaborate wedding—complete with a wedding planner and all the works. This included a $1,000 wedding cake, rented tents, an orchestra, a sit-down dinner, and the pièce de résistance . . . swans in the front yard. Many modern weddings have likewise become full-fledged productions, and couples saddle themselves with debt by throwing a one-day extravaganza that they're still paying for years later.

Fortunately, your choices aren't limited to either getting married on the front porch or spending a fortune to put on a show. You can strike a happy medium and have a memorable but not-too-costly wedding—and that's what we'll show you how to do in this chapter.

Cutting Costs—Let's Start

In chapter 1, we indicated that the average cost of a wedding is about $20,000. The cost of a wedding dress alone is somewhere between $600 and $900. The remaining arises from some of the most unsuspected sources.

Do a search on the Internet. Type in *"budgeting a wedding"* or *"saving money on your wedding."* You will find many commonsense tips. For instance, you'll find advice on using simple white table linens instead of a fancy pattern or an overlay (one tablecloth over another). If you desire color and pattern, you can add plenty with a table centerpiece. Or, rather than paying a print shop hundreds of dollars to print your wedding invitations, you can design your own invitations by purchasing a good publishing program and quality card stock. (As you make use of the suggestions, keep in mind that most Internet sites, despite good money-saving advice, project a worldly perspective.)

Creating a Wedding Budget

If you never set a boundary for costs, there will be no end to spending. Guaranteed. Creating a budget will help you determine how much things cost so you can limit your spending. It's fine to have a "wish list" of all the extras you'd love to have at your wedding, but once you have that on paper—and fill in the dollar signs by each frill—trim things off until you agree on a wedding you can afford.

There are additional wedding planning guides available on-line, sites that provide an orderly way to both plan and track costs. One great on-line resource is the "Wedding Savings System On-Line" (wedding-savings.com), which is a complete wedding planning software system that allows you to plan budget allocation, shows you cost factors involved, and gives money-saving and planning tips. Start there and look around at other sites.

About Those Rings

Rings are often huge expenses—both the engagement ring and the wedding bands. Diamonds may be a girl's best friend but those "rocks" aren't cheap. We're talking thousands of dollars for all three rings. Out of all the money you spend, this is one where you'll want to put the most thought.

If you look hard enough, you *can* find an inexpensive wedding ring for around $300. Some on-line jewelers offer something called a "starter ring" for the bargain price of $595. Ring costs are dependent on carat size, cut, and quality of the diamond. The jewelry markup can progress upwards into thousands and thousands of dollars. You can save by looking for rings on sale.

Jeff bought Teena's engagement/wedding ring set
through the Navy Exchange catalog while serving in the military and saved a bundle. If either of you has military privileges
or know someone who does, you might explore this particular
perk. (Now, if *that* doesn't make you want to join the military,
nothing will.) You can also save by looking for jewelers who are
members of the Jewelry Discount Network. These jewelers offer
lower prices because they spend less on advertising and pass
savings on to their customers.

More Money-Saving Tips

Here are some practical money-saving tips.

1. **Book your wedding for off-season.** The most popular
   months for weddings are May, June, July, and August. Even
   September can be busy in certain states. Check with florists,
   wedding consultants, caterers, etc., to see what their slow
   seasons are. Many will give you a discount if you book during their slow season. You can also sometimes save as much
   as one-third on facility rental fees during off-season.
2. **Look for discount deals.** Retailers such as tux shops, wedding shops, florists, etc., sometimes offer discounted or free
   wedding invitations just to get you into their shop. Just
   watch out what you spend once you're in.
3. **Buy display model dresses** or dresses that haven't sold from
   the previous season.
4. **Have a friend or family member take your photos.** A word
   of caution: though this will save money, make sure the person you choose has good photography skills.
5. **Enter contests. Register for giveaways.** Many on-line wedding sites such as http://www.weddingzone.net have contests and giveaways where you can register to win valuable
   items you'd otherwise need to buy for the wedding.
6. **Borrow or rent rather than buying.** You will only wear
   your wedding dress one time—excluding photo sittings.
   Save a bundle by either renting or borrowing your wedding
   dress and tux. Rather than rent a limo, borrow a friend's
   classic car and have your friend chauffeur. On a lesser scale

you can borrow toast glasses, punch bowls, and even linens. (By the way, it's actually cheaper to rent linens than to buy paper tablecloths.)

7. **Scout for free deals.** Many churches offer their fellowship halls at a nonprofit price or for free to members or regular attendees. This is less expensive than renting a facility. (Of course, many have restrictions on dancing, etc.)

8. **Make your own.** You can often make bridal dresses and bridal party dresses for the fraction of the cost of buying ready-made ones. If friends who are gifted seamstresses, floral designers, or bakers are on your guest list, consider asking them to donate their services in lieu of a gift. And check into the cost of creating your own wedding invitations and place cards. There are many user-friendly software programs designed just for this.

9. **Get several quotes.** Prices vary greatly. Check with several sources for prices on flowers, photography, etc. It often works to your advantage to let the merchant know you're shopping around. Be sure to tell them the price you've already been quoted and ask if they can beat that.

10. **Additional savings tips.** If you plan to have printed napkins, save by ordering a minimum number of printed napkins, then buy colored napkins at a discount store. Most people don't pay attention to the imprinted napkins. Most people don't respond either so forget about the added costs of RSVP cards and use the 60 percent rule (a rule developed by a professional wedding consultant)—usually only 60 percent of those who receive invitations show up.

11. **Ask a friend to be your wedding coordinator.** Wedding coordinators make organizing easier and a good coordinator can lobby for the best prices for you, but coordinators cost money. There are two packages most wedding coordinators offer. The least costly is the "day of wedding" package, which is typically a flat fee of around $500. The coordinator is there for the rehearsal, ceremony, and reception and meets on location to ensure vendors, etc., run smoothly. With full service they handle every detail from start to finish. Fees for this package start at around $1,000 and escalate. (And that

doesn't include the vendor fees.) If all of this seems like more than your pocketbook can spare, ask one of your detail-oriented dependable friends to act as a no-cost or low-cost wedding consultant.

Even with these money-saving shortcuts, your wedding will still be expensive, so you need to start saving for it today. Below is a list of wedding expenses and costs. This doesn't include small details like guest books, bouquet holders, keepsake and decoration novelties, etc. Remember, these hidden costs add up. Budget *every* item to help you see where you can cut back.

In years past the bride's family traditionally paid most of the wedding costs but today just about anything goes. In modern society, the bride and groom themselves are often expected to pay for much of their own wedding. Maybe Mom and Pop will be generous by throwing in the honeymoon and *perhaps* (if they feel like it) part of the wedding costs or maybe a new piece of furniture.

Remember that the approximate costs listed below depend on quantity, vendor prices, style, and more. Look over this list with your fiancé and then discuss it with your parents. Who knows? Maybe they're feeling generous.

Wedding Items and Approximate Costs

	Approx. Cost	Budget
The marriage license	(Varies)	
Rehearsal gifts for bride and groom	$50	_____
Rings	$1,800	_____
Personal stationery	$50–100	_____
Bride's bouquet/corsage	$50–110	_____
Bridesmaids' luncheon	$15 ea	_____
Corsages for mothers	$9–12 ea	_____
Boutonnieres for the men in wedding party	$7–8 ea	_____
Physical exam and blood test	$150 ea	_____
Gifts for parents	$50–100	_____
Gifts for groomsmen/attendants	$15 each	_____
Special wedding attire (tuxes)	$50–100	_____
Fee for the minister	$50–150	_____
The honeymoon	$2,500+	_____
Wedding coordinator	$500+	_____
Wedding cake	$2–4/serving	_____

Reception:

	Approx. Cost	Budget
Food and beverages	$8/a head	_____
Flowers/decorations	$200	_____
Gratuities for servers, DJ, etc. (dependent on rehearsal, dinner, total tab)	varies	_____
Wedding gift for the newlyweds	$50–100	_____
Bride's wedding attire	$600	_____
Bride's trousseau	$200	_____
Wedding invitations, thank-you notes, announcements, and postage	$250–400	_____
Engagement & wedding photos	$500–1,000	_____
Videographer	$1450–2450	_____

The Ceremony:

	Approx. Cost	Budget
Rental of sanctuary	$50–150	_____
Fees for musicians	$50–150	_____
Aisle runners	$29–49	_____
Altar flowers	$57–150	_____
Pew bows & additional decorations	$18–25 ea	_____
Bridesmaids' bouquets	$25–45 ea	_____
Transportation: bridal party to ceremony and to reception	$250	_____

Attendants are expected to pay for: Their own wedding attire and formal wear, travel and hotel expenses for the wedding, bridal shower and bachelor party, and a wedding gift for the couple.

CHAPTER 6

The Honeymoon and Beyond

"Yeahhh . . . a nice slow cruise to Hawaii, with maybe a week on each island, then we fly to Australia and spend a week or so there . . . and then . . ."

The Honeymoon and Beyond

Your Honeymoon

Chapter 1 listed the average cost of a wedding as $20,000, but this didn't include the cost of your honeymoon. Unquestionably, the honeymoon is *the* major highlight for newlyweds. Honeymoons can cost anywhere from a few hundred to several thousand dollars.

If you and your partner would be just as thrilled with a trip to Disneyland as a trip to Barbados, then by all means go for the simpler package. Booking your wedding (hence your honeymoon) off-season can also save big bucks. For instance, Florida vacations are often less expensive when you book between September and May. Hawaii is a popular honeymoon destination, but it's *very* expensive. There are other very nice and much less expensive destinations.

If you belong to an auto club, visit their local office. Most provide travel coordination as a benefit to members. You can obtain brochures, maps, and travel options. If you don't belong to an auto club, you can save by buying comprehensive package deals through travel agencies. Look for discount airfare on sites like travelcity.com and priceline.com. You can save even more by buying complete packages, which include transportation, hotel, and dining—and by going off-season when rates are lowest. You can even borrow a friend's cottage or cabin for an inexpensive getaway.

Unless parents have offered this expense as a gift, assume that you yourselves are footing the bill. If that's the case, be mindful that the less you spend lavishly feeding several hundred wedding guests, the *more* you can spend on a honeymoon you both will remember for the rest of your lives.

After the Honeymoon

Honeymoons are great fun, but unless you married royalty you'll have to return to the real world afterwards, set up house, and earn a living. This is when the adventure begins as you work together to make your home the way you like it. While you were on your honeymoon, you probably wined and dined each other with little thought of cooking. Back on planet Earth the transition away from eating out is tough but *has* to be made.

When a family of four recently moved halfway across the country, their belongings (including pots, pans, and utensils) were delayed for two and a half weeks due to severe weather and high customer volume. Their normal budget for food for that time frame was nearly tripled since they had to eat out. Just one trip to a fast-food establishment represents two to three meals when purchased in groceries. Multiply that for several meals over numerous days and expenses add up quickly!

Many newlyweds go out for meals instead of cooking at home because neither one knows how to cook. You not only dine at home for a *fraction* of the cost of eating out, but it's often much healthier. That's not to say that you'll be an expert cook right off the bat, but cooking is a skill that can be learned. Hey! Check through your wedding gifts again. You probably received at least half a dozen cookbooks.

Be Patient

Newlyweds Larry and Jan were a fun-loving couple whose lifestyle appealed to many of their friends. Whenever guests came to dinner, Larry enjoyed showing off his "toys," whether it was a new sound system, his latest hot car, or even the couple's posh furniture. Unknown to their admirers, Jan and Larry's fetish for acquiring "things" was burying them under debt. Several months later the cracks in Larry and Jan's façade started to show when Larry frantically began selling off many of their possessions to keep creditors at bay. He even put his cherished new Harley-Davidson up for sale.

But it was too little too late. Larry and Jan focused so much on material possessions and social status, they neglected their own marriage. Jan filed for divorce and shortly after, Larry filed for bankruptcy. They lost it all, because they didn't live within their means.

If you insist on going up to your eyeballs in debt to furnish your new house and have everything perfect as you start your new life together, you'll put huge strains on your relationship. Furnishing a home takes time; so don't expect to live the lifestyle of the rich and famous on a basic needs salary. Don't even expect to have what your *parents* have! It not only takes *knowledge* to fill rooms with "rare and beautiful treasures" (Proverbs 24:4) but money and time.

Sales departments know the attitudes of Americans today. That's the reason you see so many furniture, electronic, and department store ads in daily newspapers. If all of the ads were removed, the average newspaper would be less than half its printed length. And guess what! A *majority* of the ads are targeted specifically at young adults like you! Common hooks such as: "0 down, no payments for 12 months", or "0% financing—guaranteed credit approval" appeal to the widespread belief that "I deserve it now" and "I'll buy on credit, enjoy it now, and pay later."

More Ways to Save

- Buy in large quantities. Generally, the larger the quantity, the more you save. Get with friends and buy in bulk or join a savings club store.
- Combine errands to save on gas.
- Buy on sale. Most stores have seasonal sales when they discount items. A furniture store may have a fall clearance sale. Department stores frequently have a spring linen sale.
- Buy used furniture, clothes, and cars (*used,* not dilapidated).
- Use less laundry detergent. You rarely need the full amount.
- Buy classic clothes that won't go out of style as quickly.
- Check out www.stretcher.com for money-saving tips.
- And by all means, read the book in this series, *Personal Budgeting*.

The Danger of Buying on Credit

Because it is *such* a strong temptation for young couples to borrow huge amounts of money to get "set up" in their new home, and the chances are you will *personally* be tempted to do that as well, let's spend a little time on this whole subject of newlyweds and debt. Today it isn't unusual for young married couples to owe—with home mortgages, school loans, and car loans—$100,000 or more within the first two years of marriage. Although this is the *norm* in our society, it is *not* what God plans for us. (See Psalm 37:21; Romans 13:8.)

If the average young married couple looked closely to what makes up their collective debts, they would probably learn a cold, hard truth: that they lean toward—or fully fall into—the category of people who want to fill up their houses with treasures but don't have the savings or money to do so debt free. Why do they do this? They have bought into the lie that they "need" and "deserve" their own private chunk of heaven on earth, and that going into debt is the expected and normal way to get that.

This doesn't mean you shouldn't ever borrow money for purchases—after all, even a home mortgage is a debt—but you should avoid borrowing to buy consumables like gifts, vacations, and clothes. OK, let's get down to the nitty-gritty.

- ***Debt is not normal:*** "Let no debt remain outstanding, except the continuing debt to love one another" (Romans 13:8). Borrowing is never God's best intention for His people. If you owe debts, pay them off faithfully.

- ***The borrower has an absolute commitment to repay:*** Many borrowers discover that it is possible for them to accumulate far more debt than they can repay and still maintain the lifestyle they want. Over one million people a year now choose bankruptcy as a way to postpone or avoid repayment. For a Christian, any loan is a vow to repay. "It is better not to vow than to make a vow and not fulfill it" (Ecclesiastes 5:5).

Keeping Your Lifeboat Afloat

Think of the scenario of surviving a shipwreck. You are given an imaginary list of items salvaged from the wreck and are asked to prioritize them in order of value. Fortunately, a rubber raft is one of the items. Imagine Jan and Larry in the same scenario. They might have tossed canteens of water overboard and opted for gourmet coffee beans instead. Couples with financial savvy know what is crucial for survival and allot money to expenses such as groceries, electricity, phone, etc., before spending on frills such as entertainment or a new dining room table. If you want to be a survivor, you must use good sense. Ask yourself, "Is this a *want* or a *need?* What would I take on life's proverbial raft?" Too often wants win out over actual needs.

Not too far from a young couple's rental home was a new development of wealthy, showier homes. They enjoyed walking through that posh neighborhood, dreaming of owning such a home themselves. Each time they walked through that development, they became more disgruntled and depressed upon returning to their humble dwelling. Soon they were sprinkling their conversation with, "I wish we had a mudroom" or "If only we had a walk-in pantry."

This mind-set began affecting their spending habits as they focused on buying nice "things" that they couldn't always afford. One day, the young woman realized the trap they had set for themselves. After talking it over, they reached the decision that if they were going to wrestle with materialism whenever they took walks in the "nice" neighborhood, they'd do better not to walk there at all. By cutting out the temptation, they could more easily deal with their spending desires.

You can do the same thing. If going to the mall causes you to spend money, take a walk through the park instead. Take every thought captive (2 Corinthians 10:5). Pay attention to what you are telling yourself about money and material possessions. When you desire something you don't need, be honest and say "I want" instead of "I need." You'll soon realize the distinction of when you are being selfish and when you really do need something. This simple perspective can be a fence that keeps you from falling into the bottomless pit of debt.

CHAPTER 7

Home Sweet Home

"Here it is . . . a great way to save money after we're married . . . whadda' ya' think?"

Home Sweet Home

Are You a Candidate for Home Ownership?

Only a few years ago it was pretty standard procedure for couples to purchase a home at the time of their wedding so they'd have a place to live after marriage. These days, however, couples are more likely to spend a minimum of four years in apartments or rented houses before they're able to save up the money for a down payment on their first home. This "waiting period" gives you the opportunity to figure out what kind of place is best suited for your tastes and needs.

Should You Rent or Buy?

Renting is often less expensive than buying—but not always—and when an appliance breaks or a roof leaks, you simply call the landlord; if you decide you want to find a new place, you have the freedom to relocate without all the time and hassle involved in selling a home. On the other hand, when you rent you sink money into someone *else's* property, plus you have limited freedom when it comes to making changes and improvements. Home ownership gives you much more freedom and builds equity. (Most homes increase in value by about 5 percent a year.)

Home ownership is a wise investment if you intend to live in the same place for a substantial amount of time and your mortgage payment, interest, taxes, and insurance do not exceed 30 percent of your net spendable income—meaning, after giving to God and paying taxes. If you plan to purchase, you're looking at a cost, on a national average, of about $100,000. Actual cost depends on where you live. The home you buy in the San Francisco Bay Area, if sold, could yield two and a half homes for one you buy in Warren, Pennsylvania.

When You're Starting Out

You may want a home with atmosphere, a gothic, fog-enshrouded manor house with ancient ivy-covered masonry. Your mate may be hoping for a sprawling ranch house in a twelve-choice color range. But remember when you're newly married, you can't "have it all" instantly unless you plan to go in debt way, *way* over your heads. Translated into real time this means that not only can't you buy all the "dream" furniture, stereos, and giant TVs you want—now and right now—but you're *also* not going to be able to buy your dream house to put all that furniture in.

When you're starting out, chances are good you'll be renting. Seeing as how you'll have just paid for your wedding, your rings, and your honeymoon, it's a fair assumption to make that you probably won't have enough money left to buy your ultimate dream house. If you've saved up enough money for the down payment of a modest house—or even a "starter" house—you're doing well. You have to live within your budget, and to do *that* you need to "have learned the secret of being content in any and every situation" (Philippians 4:12). We live in a generation that demands instant gratification and is willing to go deep into debt to get satisfaction, but this is neither godly nor realistic.

Start a Savings Plan

The initial down payment for a home, as stated before, is usually a minimum of 10 percent of the total cost. (For the remaining 90 percent, couples normally take out a mortgage.) Most young couples don't have an extra $10,000 lying around, so how are many people able to own homes? They save up the money, slowly, faithfully over the months and years. "He who gathers money little by little makes it grow" (Proverbs 13:11). This takes self-discipline and means saying no to a lot of instant gratifications—vacations, meals out, movies—that would gobble up that cash. Keep reminding each other of your dream of owning a house.

One of the best things you can do is to open a Home Owners Savings Plan. Phone different banks and ask about the types of plans they have to offer. Also keep in mind that in addition to the down payment, there are the additional fees and closing costs of home buying (2 to 5 percent). So let's say that all told you need 15 percent (or $15,000) saved up before you can buy a home. If your goal is to buy a home in five years, you'd have to save $5,000 a year, or about $415/month. Can you *do* it? Yes, if you want to bad enough.

By the way, the more you put down in your down payment, the less interest you'll pay out over the life of your mortgage. Most institutions require a down payment of between 5 to 20 percent. The lower down payment options are usually reserved for first-time buyers. However, the more you put down up front, the smaller your loan will be and the lower your monthly mortgage payments.

For More Information

If you don't have the finances in place yet to buy a home, then of course you'll have to rent. If so, we recommend that you purchase the other book in this series, *Renting Your First Apartment*. This book gives a wealth of practical advice on how to mange all the details and find the right apartment for you.

If you *do* have enough money saved up to make the down payment on a home and are seriously into the house-hunting market, we strongly urge you to read the other book in this series, *Buying Your First House*. The information there can save you megaheadaches and many thousands of dollars— maybe even tens of thousands of dollars.

A word of caution: Although financial institutions are now allowing people to "buy" homes with no down payment at all, the interest you will pay as a result is enormous. We strongly discourage "buying" a home that way. The best method is to save up money for a down payment ahead of time, then get into a house.

CHAPTER 8

Bills and Savings

Bills and Savings

Budgeting—A Financial Foundation

In the last chapter we talked about saving up for one of the biggest expenses you'll ever have—buying a home. We even told you just how much you'd have to squirrel away every month in order to make the down payment on a home. But how do you save the money without cannibalizing other bill payments? You need a budget. While this may not be the most fun thing you'll do as a couple, it will be one of the wisest. Set aside a weekend together when you can discuss every aspect of your family finances.

Take a look at the *Monthly Income & Expenses* chart on page 54. These categories were developed by Crown Financial Ministries and fine-tuned over the years, and while they're not carved in stone like the Ten Commandments, they are truly sound financial advice. They are tried, they are proven, and they actually work. Though the percentages may vary slightly in your personal budget, to completely disregard these guidelines is to do so at your own risk. But if you faithfully allot your money to these categories, you'll have the money to pay all your bills on time and in full.

Create a Budget

Plenty of people live from paycheck to paycheck and squeak by without a budget, true, but most of them struggle financially or are in serious debt. Why? Without a budget it's hard to know how much they're spending or can afford to spend. Not only that, it's extremely difficult to build up any savings. A budget can point out where you're wasting money, can keep you focused on goals, and curb impulse buying.

Make a couple photocopies of the *Monthly Income & Expenses* chart, complete one as a guideline to estimate, as accurately as possible, what your monthly spending will be like after you're married. What you agree—and don't agree—on will give you a clear understanding of each other's spending habits

50

and where you'll need to make adjustments. (And don't forget to do actual budgets once you're married and compare them to these estimates.)

The NSI (Net Spendable Income), not the gross income, is used to calculate the ideal spending for each budget category. Your NSI is what you have left to spend after giving to God and paying your taxes. If you know actual tax amounts, use those. For example, a couple with combined incomes of $25,000 per year will pay about 19 percent (including federal and state) of their gross income. For more information on determining your current Federal tax rate, visit the IRS website at http://www.irs.gov/.

Bill-Paying Priorities

Let's go through the list and determine which bills are top priorities and must be paid first.

1. *Giving to God.* First, give to God. This shows that you acknowledge that everything in your life comes from God.
2. *Paying your rent.* If you don't pay your rent, you're out on the street and your credit record takes a big dent.
3. *Regular bills.* These include your monthly electric bill; your gas, water, and phone bills; car payments; and debts (such as credit card payments). And if you have any other bills, now is the time to pay them.
4. *Groceries.* Yes, food is fourth in line, not first. If you stick to your budget and don't make unbudgeted expenses, you should have 17 percent of your income left for food.
5. *Transportation.* This is money for gas or your bus pass. Fifteen percent of your income is earmarked Auto so if you don't have a car, put this money in a savings account for the day you'll want to buy one.
6. *Medical expenses.* Five percent of your income should go here.
7. *Saving for a house.* Set aside money each month to reach your goal of paying the down payment on a house.
8. *Savings.* If you faithfully put 5 percent of your budget into savings, you'll be able to finance purchases—like a new couch, etc.—with cash.
9. *Clothing.* Need new clothes? Now's the time to buy them.
10. *Entertainment/recreation.* If you have any money left over,

use it here. According to the budget, you should have 7 percent of your income left. If not, you've spent it somewhere else.

Set a regular monthly time for paying bills and then choose one of you to manage them. The best way to get organized is to set up an accordion folder where you keep all receipts from that particular month's expenditures. Tally them up at month's end and record them in your budget sheet. Then put the receipts and paid bills into files by category. Suggested categories would be phone, utilities, car, etc. Likewise, have a place for bills. Once these bills have been paid for the month, they should be added to the categorized folders.

Your Savings Plan

When you say, "I do," you not only pledge to love and cherish each other for the long term; by committing yourself to your marriage, you are *also* committing to some long-term expenses that require months, even years of saving. (Your dream of a house, for example.) The only way you'll have the money to meet these needs is if you start saving now. If you *don't* commit to saving, you'll still have your partner to kiss, but you'll be kissing everything else good-bye—including buying a home, college for your kids, new furniture, and more.

You'll notice on the budget that your savings should average 5 percent of your available income. This is clearly not enough when you consider all the major things you need to save money for—such as an emergency reserve fund, buying a home, your children's future, etc.—but it is a good place to *start*. In another book in this series, *Your First Savings Plan,* we show you exactly where to get all that money. We highly recommend that you purchase and study that book. But for now, commit yourself to setting aside 5 percent of your paycheck into a savings account.

Emergency Reserve Fund

This should be your first savings priority. This fund is to be used for genuine emergencies. This is not a "slush fund" to be used for financing a skiing trip or a new couch. This is for genuine, unforeseen emergencies. No matter how tight finances are, you should be able to set aside a few dollars per week. Your goal should be to build up an amount equal to at least three months' income. Keep your money in a secure fund where resources can be easily converted to cash without an early withdrawal penalty. Banks, credit unions, and money market mutual funds are the best choices for this type of fund.

Short-Range Savings Goals

A short-term goal is something that you have to save toward for a few months—or even one year—to buy. If you need a new couch, microwave oven, or some other not-so-expensive (but not-so-cheap) item, and there's not enough money in your budget to pay for it this month, you'll have to save for it. If you want a $100 leather jacket but *your* half of the clothing budget only allows you to spend $50 a month, you'll need to save your clothing money for two months to buy that jacket. Although you can get instant gratification by purchasing on buy-now-pay-later plans, by the time you've paid all the interest payments, you'll have paid more than that item was worth. So save, then buy.

Long-Range Savings Goals

Long-term expenses are goals you must save towards for a couple of years—or even decades—to reach. These include some of your personal dreams and goals that will take you toward your life's vision. The dollar amounts for some of these goals are huge, and it takes a long time to save money for them. But with patience and time, these goals are reachable. They include: (1) buying a home, (2) buying a new car when your present one dies, (3) money toward your children's education, (4) retirement savings, (5) your personal dreams and goals. This last category includes anything from a thirty-foot boat to a dream vacation to taking a two-month missions trip.

For some of these, you're going to want to put your money somewhere where it's a little more aggressive in its earning power than a regular savings account. For that, you will need to invest your money. (For more detailed information on that, see another book in this series, *Planning Your First Investment*.)

Monthly Income & Expenses

Annual Income	_____	**7. Debts (5%)**	_____
Monthly Income	_____	Credit Cards	_____
		Loans & Notes	_____
		Other	_____
LESS			
1. Charitable Giving	_____	**8. Enter. / Recreation (7%)**	_____
2. Tax	_____	Eating Out	_____
		Trips	_____
NET SPENDABLE INCOME	_____	Baby-sitters	_____
		Activities	_____
3. Housing (30%)	_____	Vacation	_____
Mortgage (Rent)	_____	Other	_____
Insurance	_____		
Taxes	_____	**9. Clothing (5%)**	_____
Electricity	_____		
Gas	_____	**10. Savings (5%)**	_____
Water	_____		
Sanitation	_____	**11. Medical Expenses (5%)**	_____
Telephone	_____	Doctor	_____
Maintenance	_____	Dental	_____
Other	_____	Drugs	_____
		Other	_____
4. Food (17%)	_____		
		12. Miscellaneous (6%)	_____
5. Auto(s) (15%)	_____	Toiletry, Cosmetics	_____
Payments	_____	Beauty, Barber	_____
Gas & Oil	_____	Laundry, Cleaning	_____
Insurance	_____	Allowances, Lunches	_____
License	_____	Subscriptions, Gifts	_____
Taxes	_____	(Incl. Christmas)	
Maint/Repair/		Special Education	_____
Replacement	_____	Cash	_____
		Other	_____
6. Insurance (5%)	_____		
Life	_____	**TOTAL EXPENSES**	_____
Medical	_____		
Other	_____	Net Spendable Income	_____
		Difference	_____

CHAPTER 9

Having Children

"... six kids ... six kids ... SIX kids? I'll need six jobs ...!"

"All I said was that we had six kids in my family, and it was great growing up with so many brothers and sisters, so why not?"

Having Children

Raising Children

Most likely your main focus right now is on your wedding and the beginning of your marriage. The thought of having children may be a proverbial "gleam in the eye." But life's pace seems to pick up after marriage, and when babies come, they bring about major changes in your lifestyle and new responsibilities.

A woman who teaches birth and infant care seminars has a poster on her wall. On the left side of the poster the caption reads, "What it takes to be a father." Beneath this heading is a picture of a sperm. The caption on the right side says, "What it takes to be a dad." Beneath this heading is a list of words such as: spend time with your children, give them love, provide a safe home, etc. How true! Anyone can have a kid but raising a child takes a lot of time and effort.

Are You Ready?

People who marry usually end up having children and raising a family. Although children are a blessing, a 1999 USDA report revealed that the estimated cost of child rearing for middle-income, two-parent families ranges from $8,450 to $9,530 annually ($152,830 over seventeen years!). Yikes! The more children you add to your family, the more spiritual, physical, and financial responsibilities you'll face. That's why careful financial planning is so crucial for creating a stable home.

Planning for the Short Term

Though you may be in great health now and don't *plan* to start a family for a while, you need to know that stuff happens. Have a serious talk with your partner about when you would like to start a family and then take the appropriate measures to make it possible. Delaying a family for a few years may be exactly what you need in order to lay a secure financial foundation.

If one of you doesn't already have a job with comprehensive health benefits, you'll either need to look for one that does or take out your own coverage. (Make sure it includes prenatal care.) This is vital, because paying out-of-pocket expenses for health benefits can run into hundreds, even thousands of dollars.

In day-to-day living, you can save on the expense of raising children by shopping for gently used clothing, exchanging outgrown clothing with friends who have children just the right age, and frequenting garage sales for everything from strollers to toy boxes. Buy end-of-season clothing on sale that is a few sizes too big.

Preparing for Long Term

Parenting is a full-time job. Children are appropriately designated as dependents. You need to be prepared to make life changes in order to care and provide for them, both now—with strollers, playpens, and adorable little outfits—as well as in the future with school necessities, braces, and prom attire. Count on a minimum of twenty years provision for each child.

Periodic review of your budget enables you to make changes, additions, and deletions that are relevant to your situation. It goes without saying that your budget for food, sundries, and clothing entries will have to increase with each additional child. So tweak your budget until it's set up to meet these needs.

The Importance of Life Insurance

Though death is not something most people like to think about, securing life insurance will make sure your future family is taken care of should something happen to the main breadwinner. This insurance provides funds to replace the financial value of the wage earner's income should something happen to that person. The amount you take out depends on the ages of your children. As a general rule, the younger your children are and the more children you have, the more you'll need. Also look at the income capability of the surviving spouse and the existing debt, current lifestyle, income, and other sources of after-death income that exist. (For more specific information on insurance, see the book in this series, *Buying Insurance*.)

Creating a Will

Many people avoid creating a will, assuming things will be somehow taken care of if they die. If, however, you die without a will, the state in which you live will distribute your assets according to their laws of *intestacy* ("the state of dying without a legal will"). What is done in one state may vary greatly from the next. Things are almost never divvied up according to the way you would have distributed them, and if you have dependents, things can get complicated.

Some things to consider include who will inherit your property if you die and who will act as guardian of your children. Without a will, should something happen to you and your spouse, in most states your children will become wards of the state. If you want to avoid that, then make a will. You should each have a will and should understand what each will dictates. Make your will a matter of prayer, then write out your wishes on paper and meet with a competent attorney who will write up a formalized will.

The Future Is Closer than You Think

Even though your children going to college is in the future, the future is closer than you think. It's never too early (but may soon be too late) to start saving for their postsecondary education. The average cost of a college education these days is $40,000. This figure will undoubtedly go up by the time your kids enroll in college twenty years from now. You must have a committed mind-set ahead of time, knowing what you're getting into.

Start now by setting a savings goal. Begin a trust fund to pay for college tuition. This will help pay everything from food and clothing to their specialized career training. In order to have a good grasp on what to put aside, consider the number of years you have before your first child starts college, how much investment risk you are willing to take, the minimum investment requirements needed in order to save the needed money, and how you can minimize the taxation amount on investment earnings.

CHAPTER 10

Here Comes the Bride

"Whoo boy . . . here we go . . . here she comes . . . I hope I'm ready for this."

"Hey, don't worry. You've prepared well for this. Enjoy your day!"

"Yeah, and I've enjoyed marriage ever since!"

Here Comes the Bride

Getting married involves much more than just buying an engagement ring. Relax. Marriage *is* a huge responsibility but no one knows it all starting out. This book is merely a helpful "heads-up" based on sound biblical principles and the experiences of other trailblazing Christian couples, and will help give you concrete and hands-on ways to be prepared.

Begin Now

Living within a budget may still be a new idea for you and your partner. Saving money might be new too. Most newlyweds start out with limited funds so don't be discouraged if you only have a few dollars to put into savings after paying bills. When you put what money you have into savings, it will produce more money—especially if you start *now* and give it time to gather interest and compound interest.

You actually need to set up two budgets. The first one is your wedding budget. Figure out all wedding costs and how much you can afford to spend on each item and category. Make sure to set a ceiling on expenses. Then you need to set up a household budget with your partner. Then, after marriage, you'll have a major building block in place.

Tenderly Hold Each Other . . . Accountable

When you agree to marry, you make an agreement to stick with each other "for better, for worse." Though the "worse" clause in those vows doesn't even seem to be in the picture right now, there will come a time when the going gets tough. That's when true commitment starts and you'll need to remember your promise to love and honor each other.

In some ways, your budget is similar to your marriage commitment and is an agreement to be accountable to each other (and to your family and creditors) for your finances. Review it frequently and confide in each other when you're having difficulty sticking with it.

Finally, it would definitely be worth your money to

check out the other titles in *The World's Easiest Pocket Guide* series to give you both a solid knowledge of biblical financial principles in every area of your new life together.

Your Premarriage Checklist

Working jointly with a spouse will take some getting used to as you each try to conform and merge your own desires, personality, and habits into one unified team. OK, here's how to start saving and preparing for the big day in a practical way. Use the list below to check off what you have done. List every expense that you will have, estimate the cost, and check it off when done.

Do Immediately

- Complete your education/career training.
- Get a good job (one with medical/dental benefits).
- Pay off existing debts (complete *Debt Work Sheet*, chapter 4).
- Set up premarital counseling.
- Discuss and set the amount of your regular giving to God.
- Rid yourselves of as many habits as possible that create debt.
- Create a wedding budget (and stick with it).
- Determine who pays for what.
- Plan and pay for your honeymoon.
- Establish a household budget.
- Determine which of you will manage the books and pay bills.
- Find a place to live within your means.
- Start communicating about finances.
- Open a savings account.
- Discuss when you would like to have children.

Do As Soon After Marriage As Possible

- Open a college savings fund for each child.
- Open savings accounts for your children.
- Buy life insurance.
- Create a will.

    Keep this pocket guide handy as well as other pocket guides and Christian financial resources in your family library. Be sure to review what you have learned from these pages. This will enable you to retain the principles and teach them to your children or others contemplating marriage. Enjoy your lives together!

Glossary

Benefits: Things you receive from an employer above and beyond salary, such as medical coverage and 401K retirement accounts.

Budget: A written plan where you allot a percentage of your income to each specific category of bills and expenses before you have the money.

Charitable giving: Giving income back to the Lord, the source of all blessing and supply (this is often a tithe of 10 percent).

Down payment: The upfront money needed when purchasing a home, usually a minimum of 10 percent of the home's total cost.

Equity: The money value of property that exceeds the loans against it.

Interest: Money you pay for the privilege of borrowing money—or receive in a savings account or investment.

Intestacy: The state of dying without leaving a legally acceptable will.

Long-range savings: Saving thousands of dollars over a period of years (or a lifetime) to meet large savings goals.

Mortgage: A lien against property that is eliminated upon full payment. (In plain English, home payments you make to the bank every month.)

Net Spendable Income (NSI): Money left over from your paycheck after charitable giving and taxes. You then budget this NSI into various categories.

Short-term savings: Savings you establish and contribute to over a period of weeks and months in order to meet a smaller and more immediate savings goal.

Stewardship: Management of the funds and resources God has given you.

Index

Larry Burkett's Stewardship for the Family™ provides the practical tips and tools that children and parents need to understand biblical principles of stewardship. Its goal is *"Teaching Kids to Manage God's Gifts—Time, Talents and Treasures."* Stewardship for the Family™ materials are adapted from the works of best-selling author on business and personal finances, **Larry Burkett**. Larry is the author of more than 60 books and hosts the radio programs *Money Matters* and *How to Manage Your Money,* aired on more than 1,100 outlets worldwide. Visit Larry's website at www.mm4kids.org